AuthorHouse™
1663 Liberty Drive
Bloomington, IN 47403
www.authorhouse.com
Phone: 1 (800) 839-8640

Published by AuthorHouse 02/04/2019

ISBN: 978-1-5462-7926-6 (sc)
ISBN: 978-1-5462-7925-9 (e)

Print information available on the last page.

authorHOUSE®

IT'S 420 SOMEWHERE

CANNABIS COLOURING BOOK

SIGNE KNUTSON

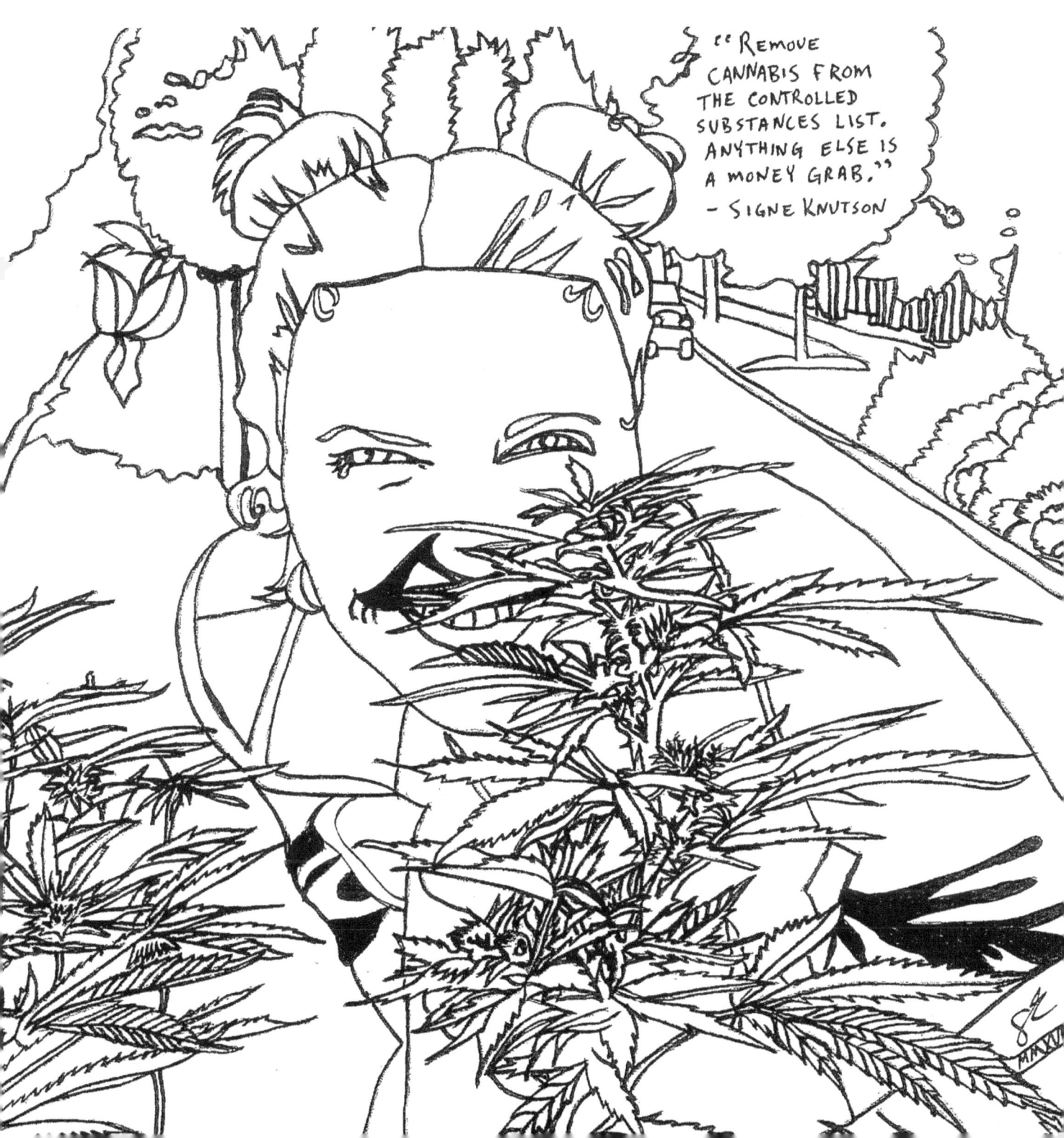

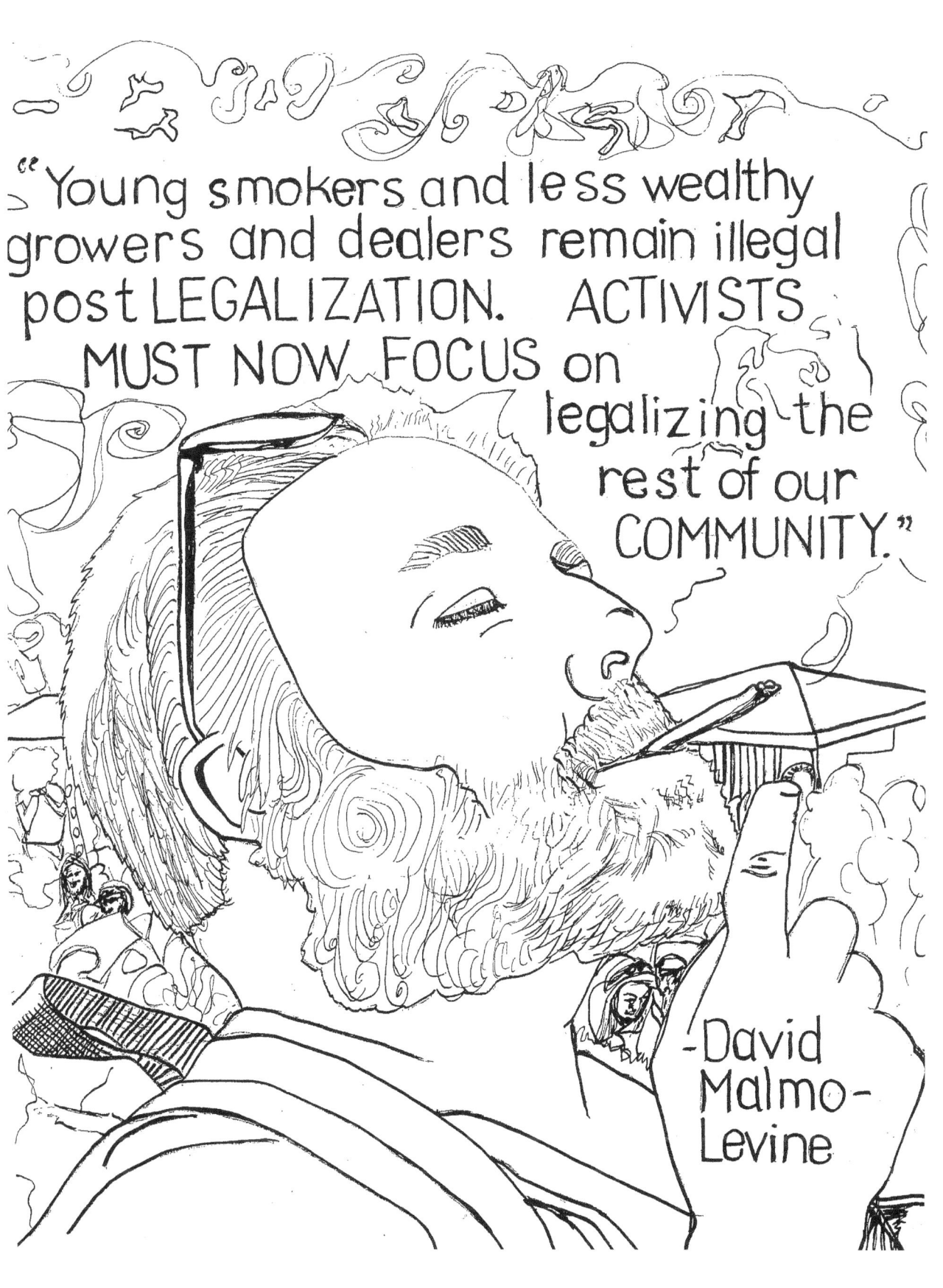

"Young smokers and less wealthy growers and dealers remain illegal post LEGALIZATION. ACTIVISTS MUST NOW FOCUS on legalizing the rest of our COMMUNITY."

-David Malmo-Levine

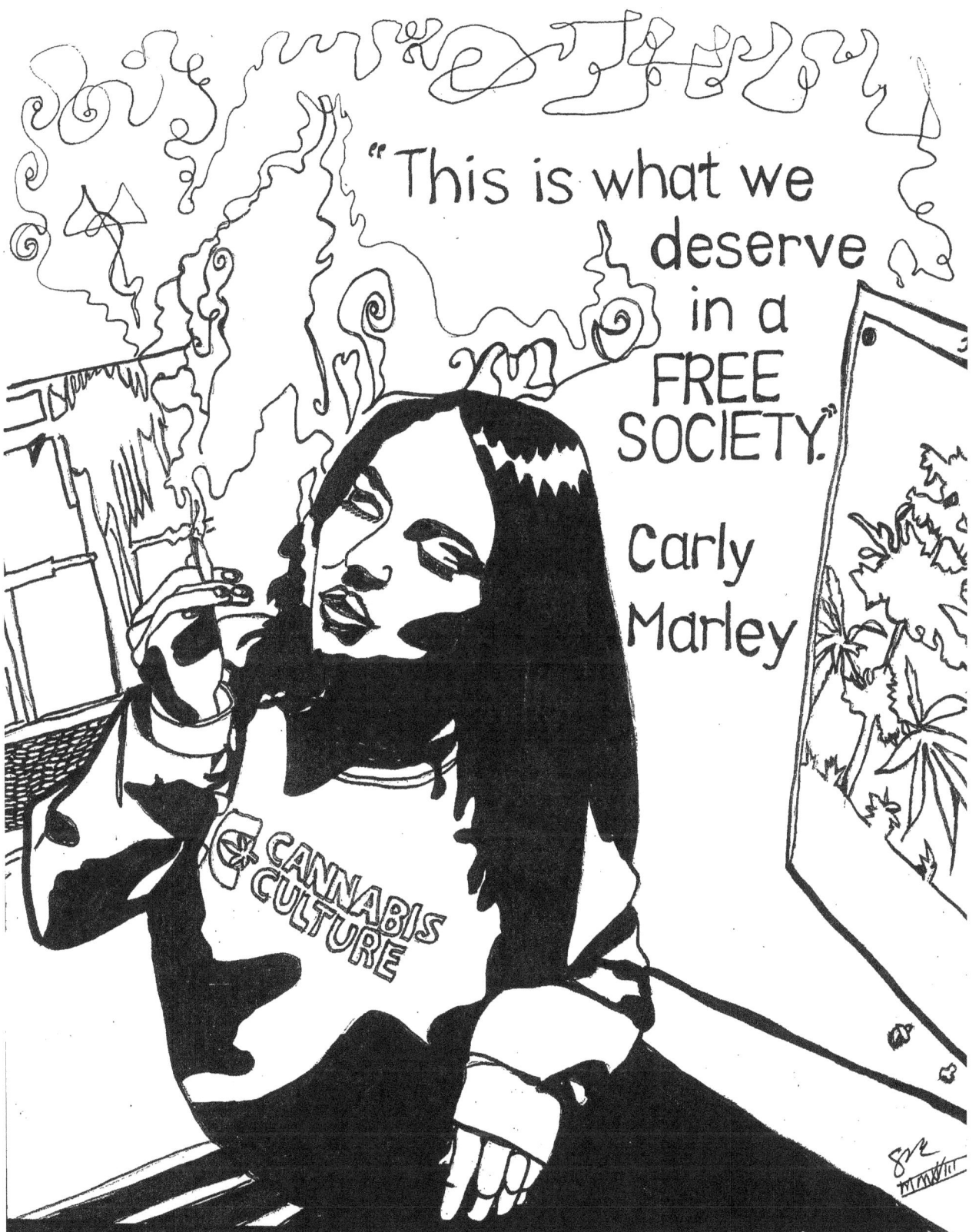

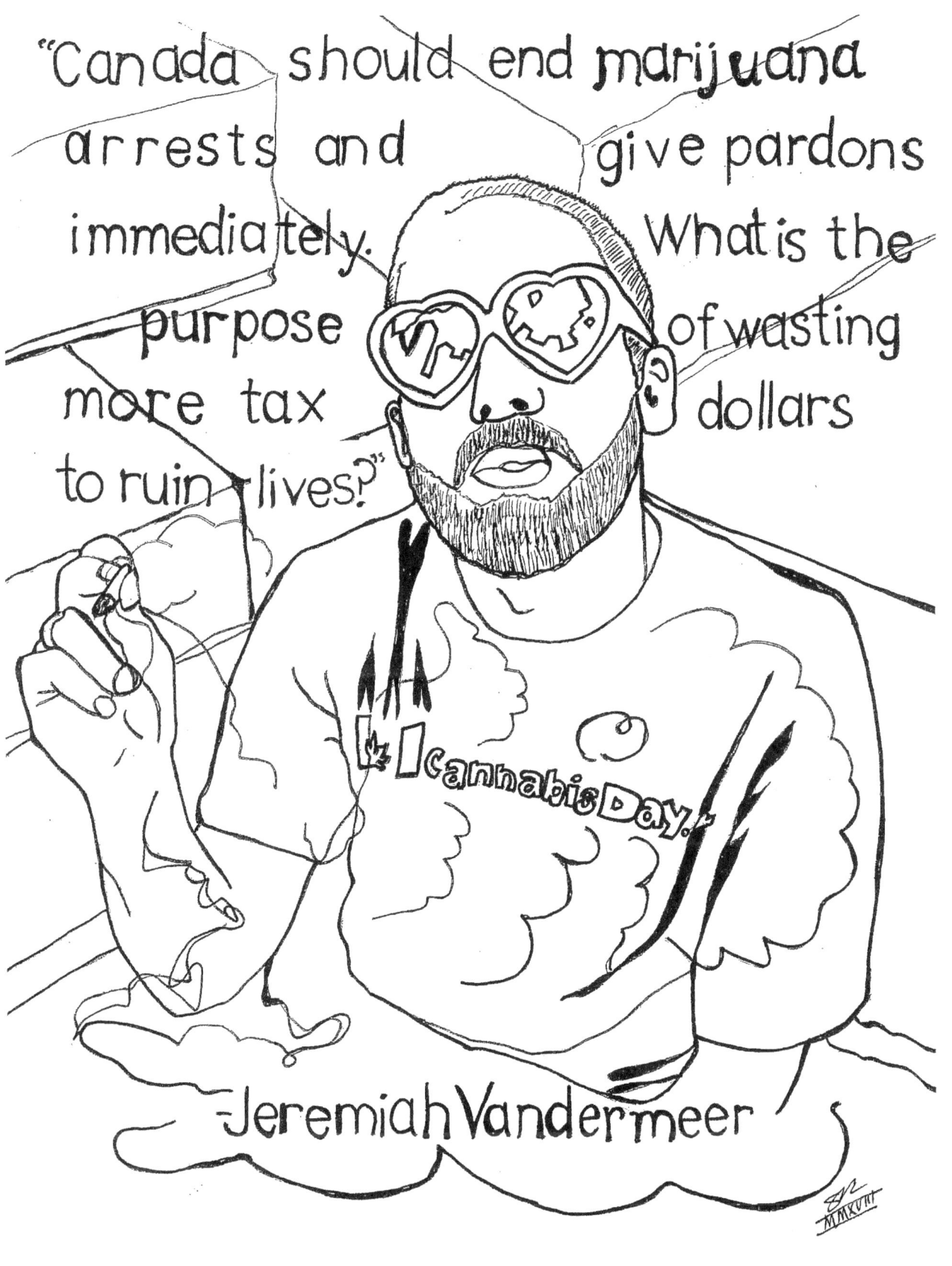

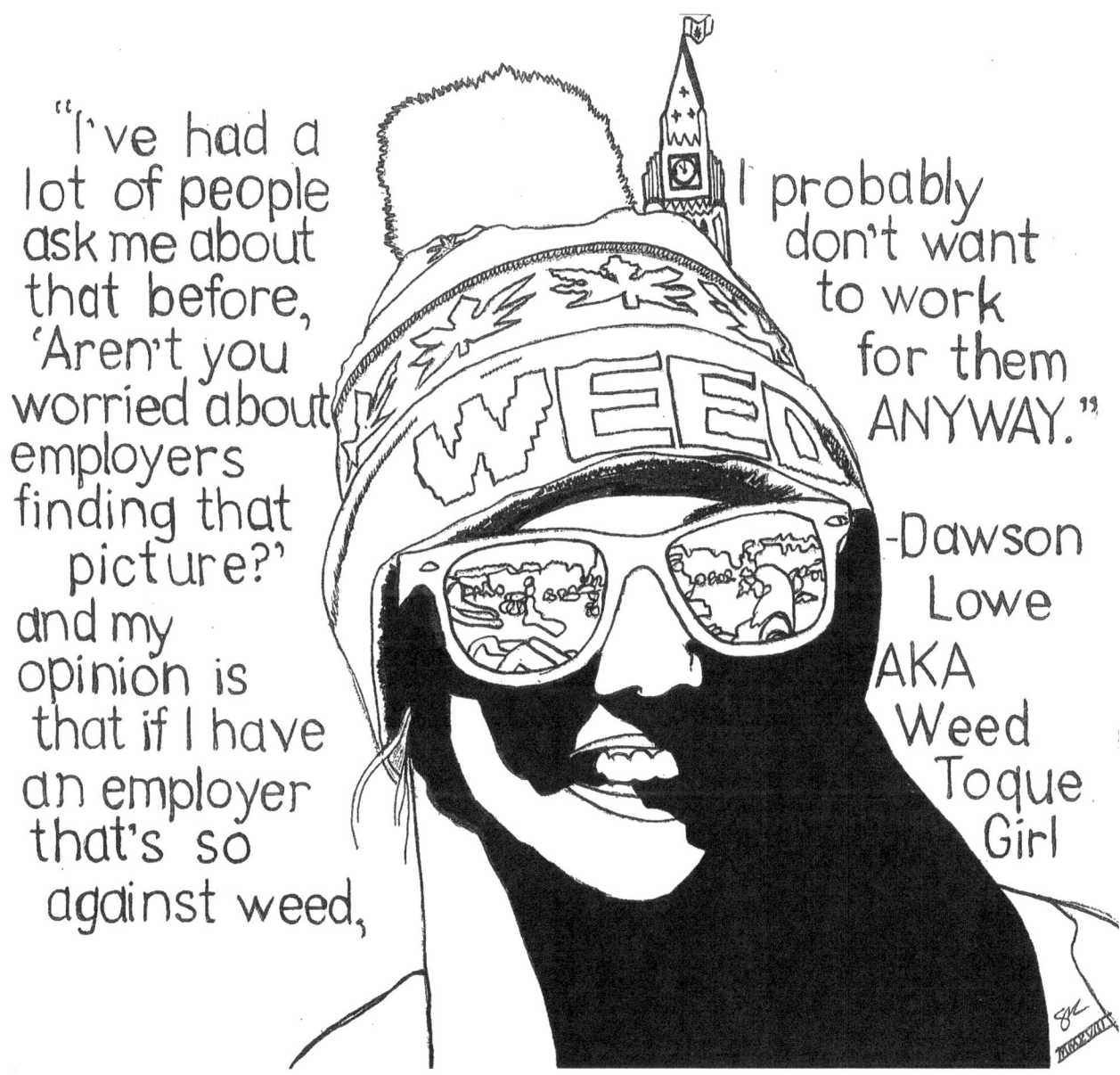

"I've had a lot of people ask me about that before, 'Aren't you worried about employers finding that picture?' and my opinion is that if I have an employer that's so against weed,

I probably don't want to work for them ANYWAY."

-Dawson Lowe AKA Weed Toque Girl

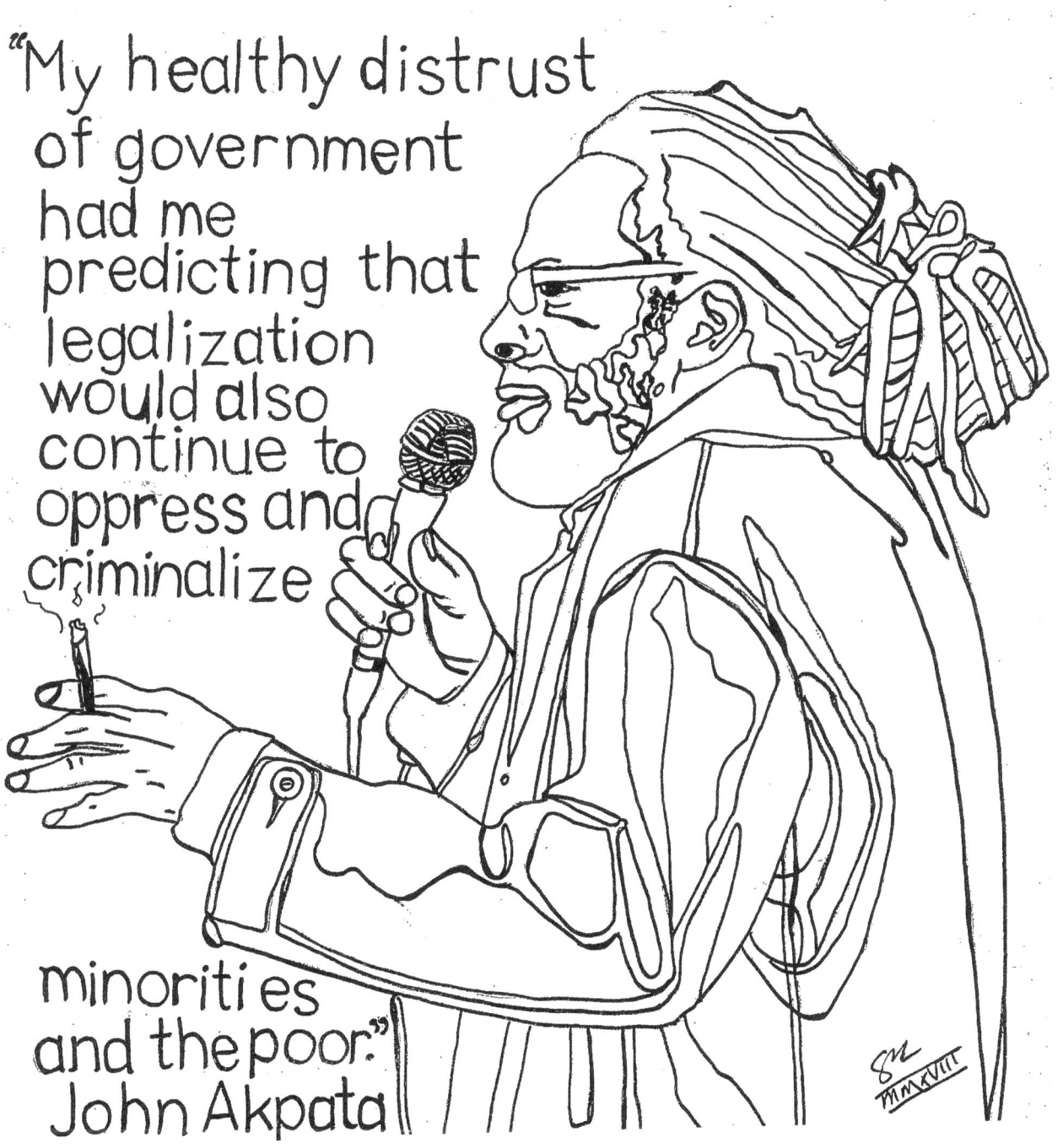

"My healthy distrust
of government
had me
predicting that
legalization
would also
continue to
oppress and
criminalize

minorities
and the poor."
John Akpata

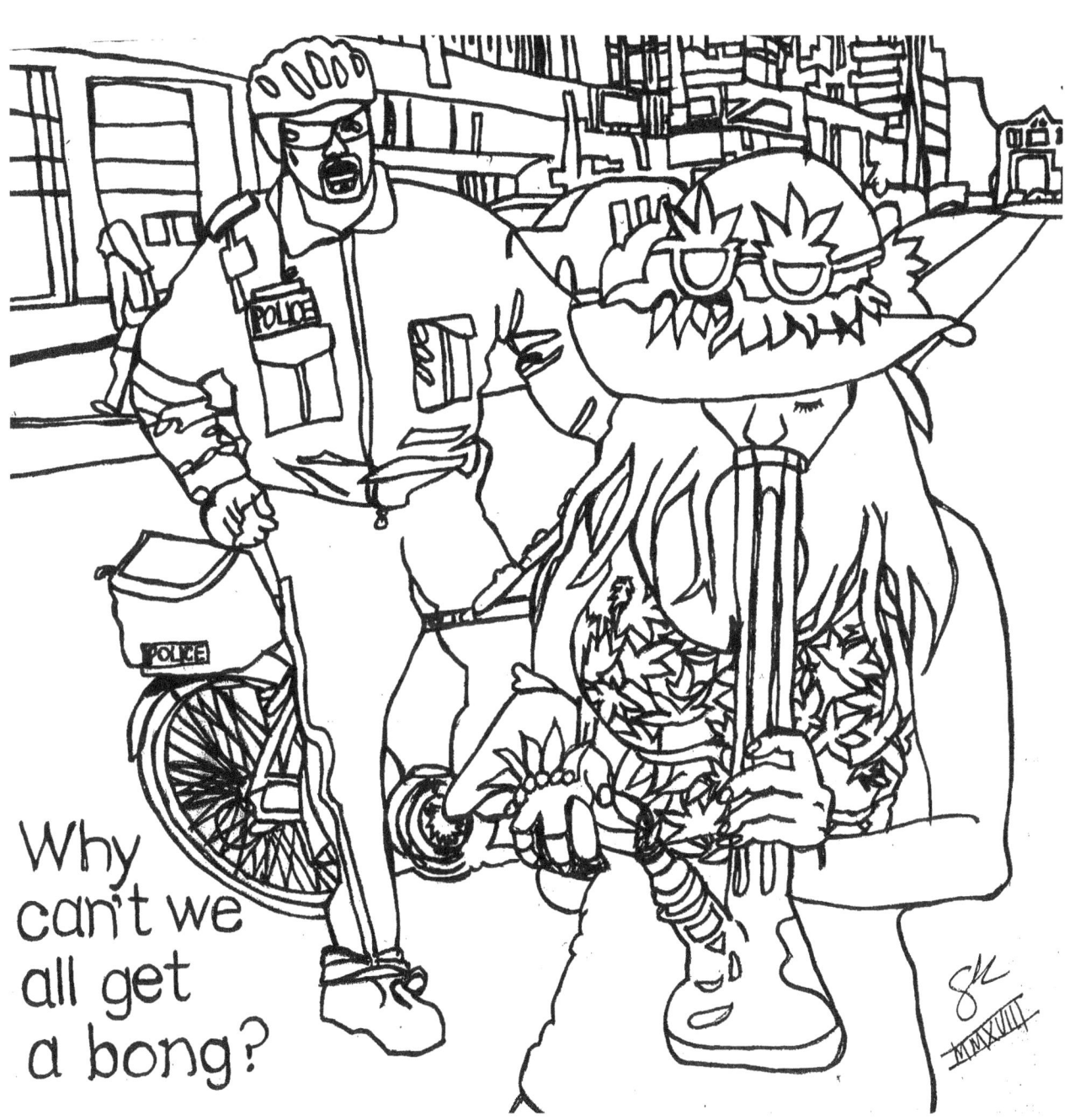

Why can't we all get a bong?

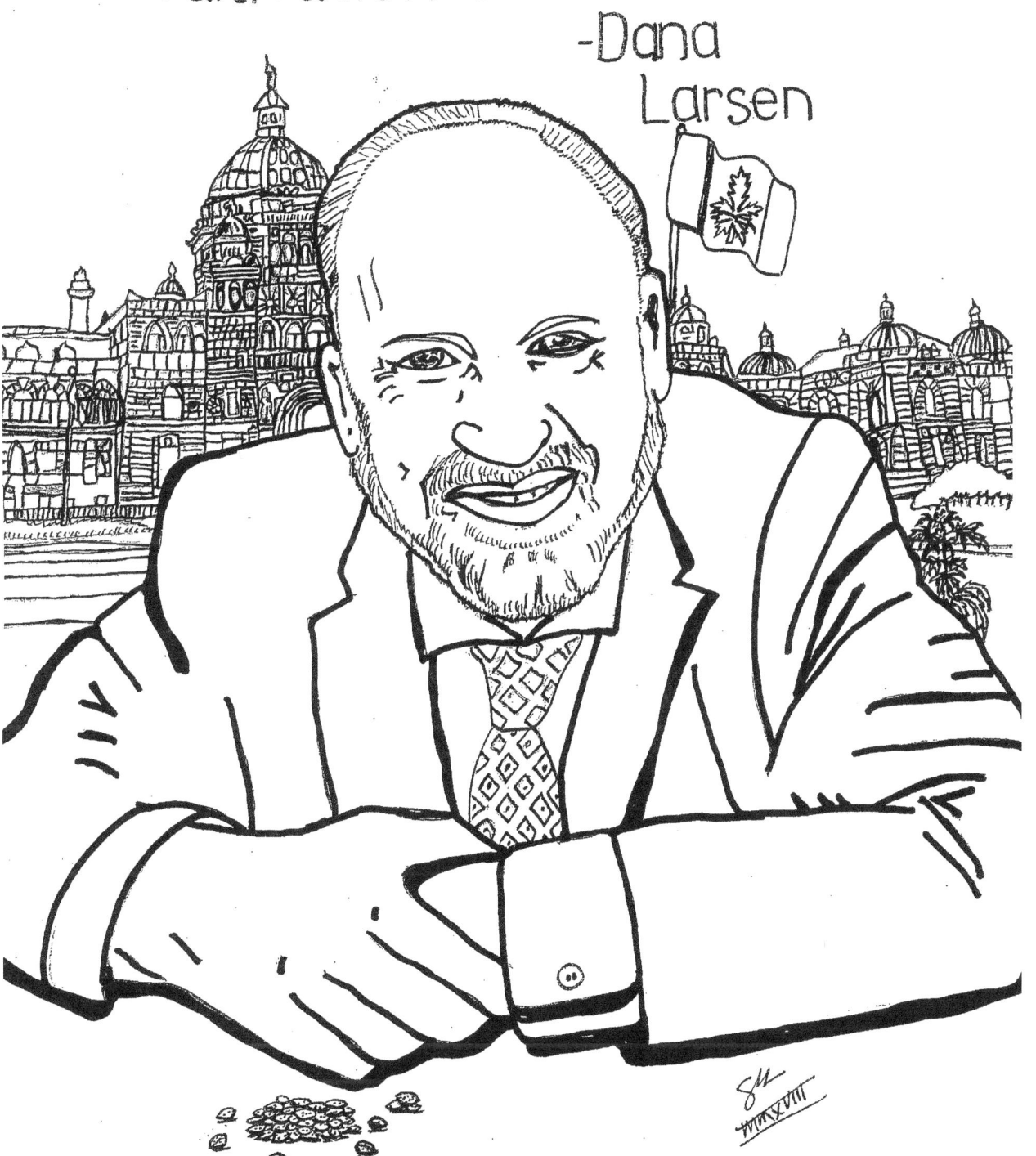

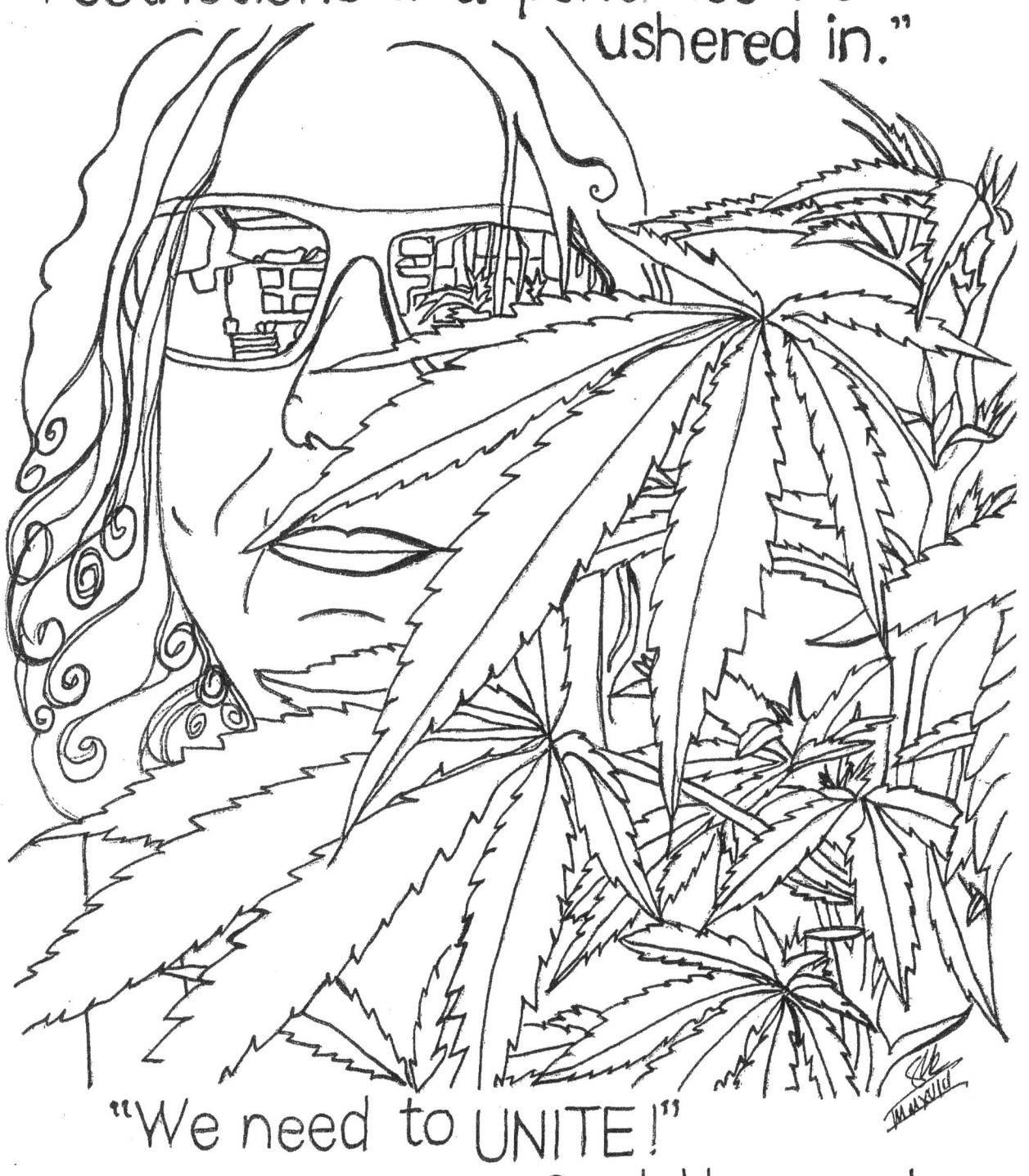

"Can't stand by and watch the restrictions and penalties be ushered in."

"We need to UNITE!"
-Cindy Heemeryk

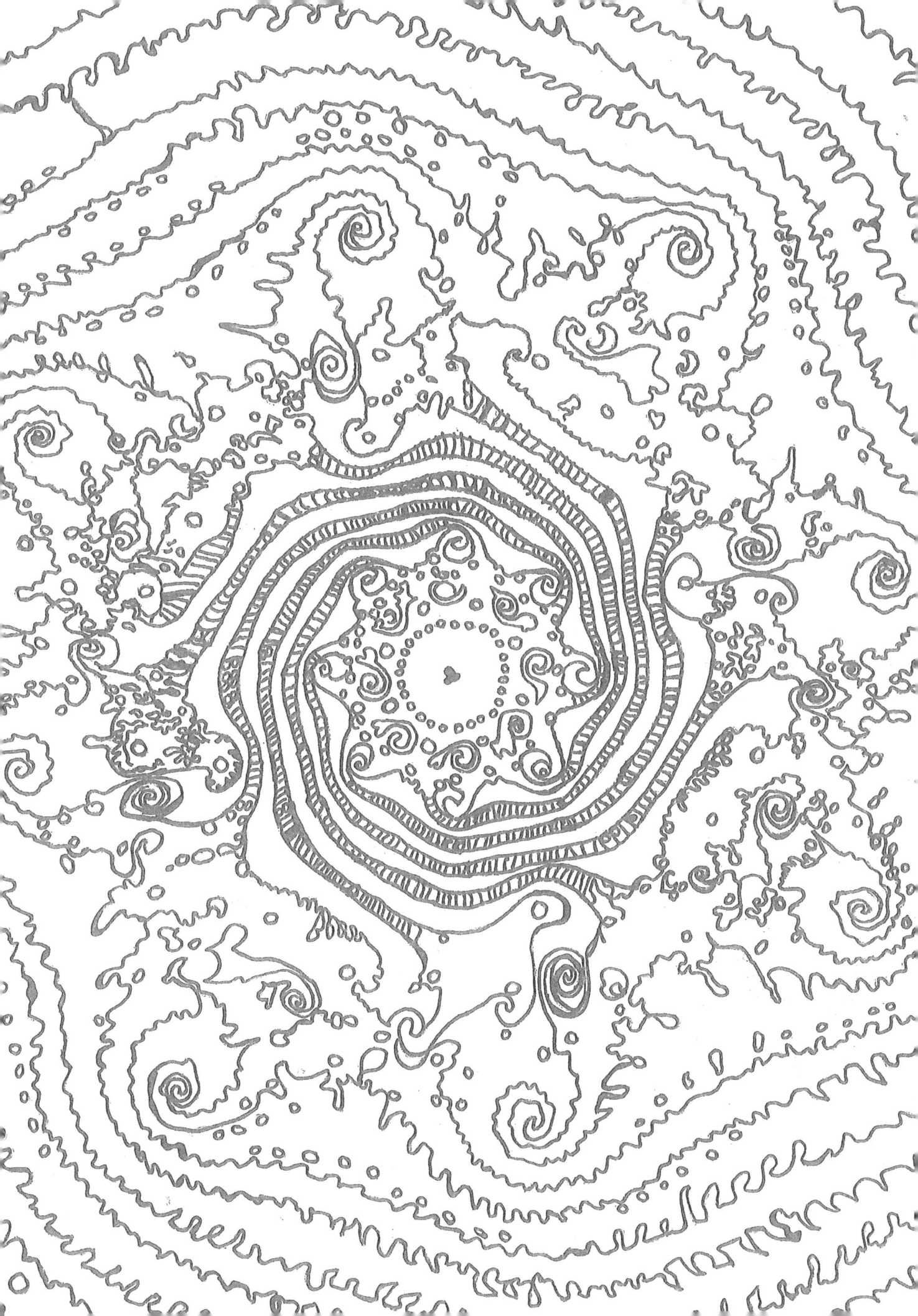

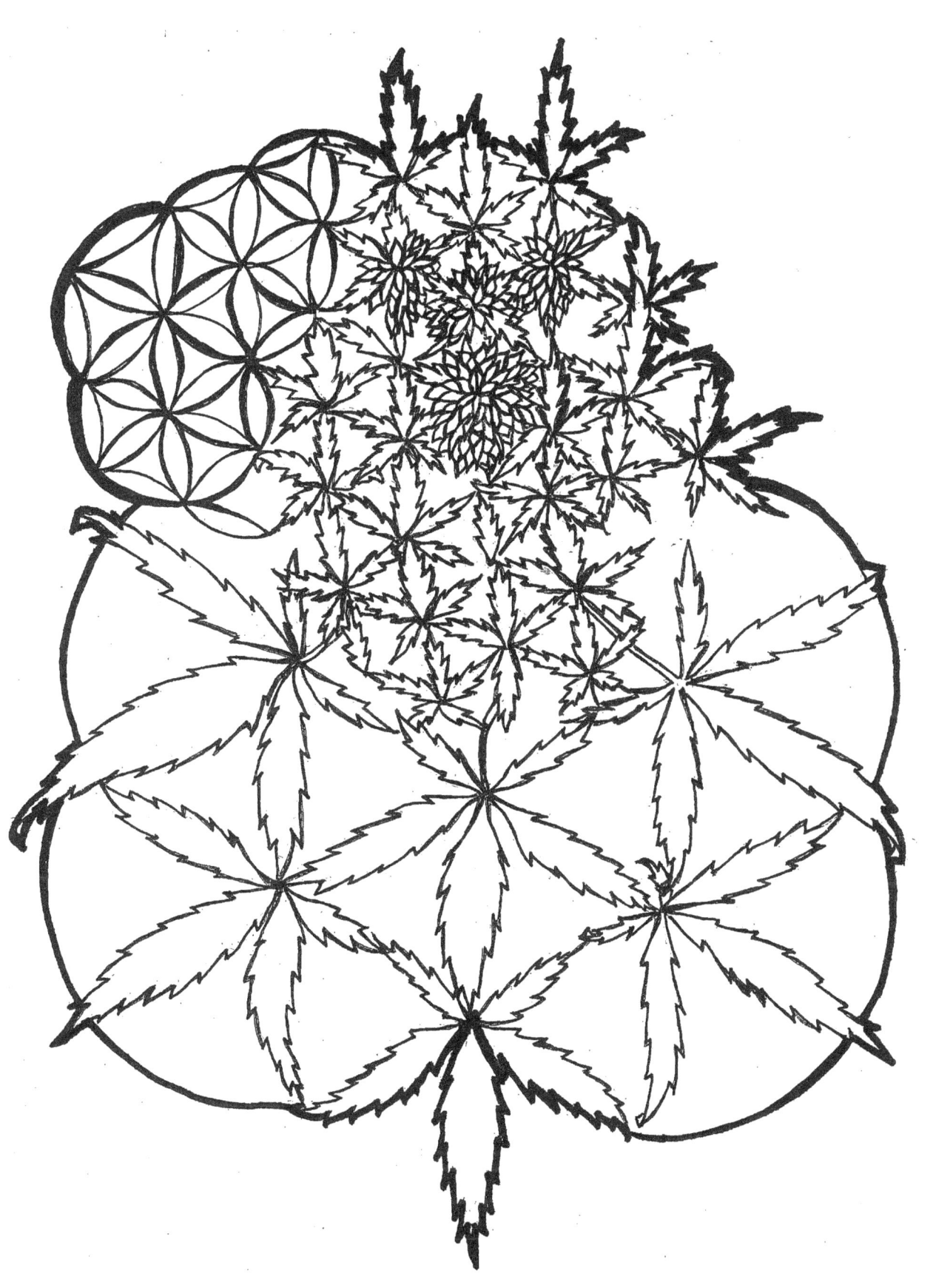

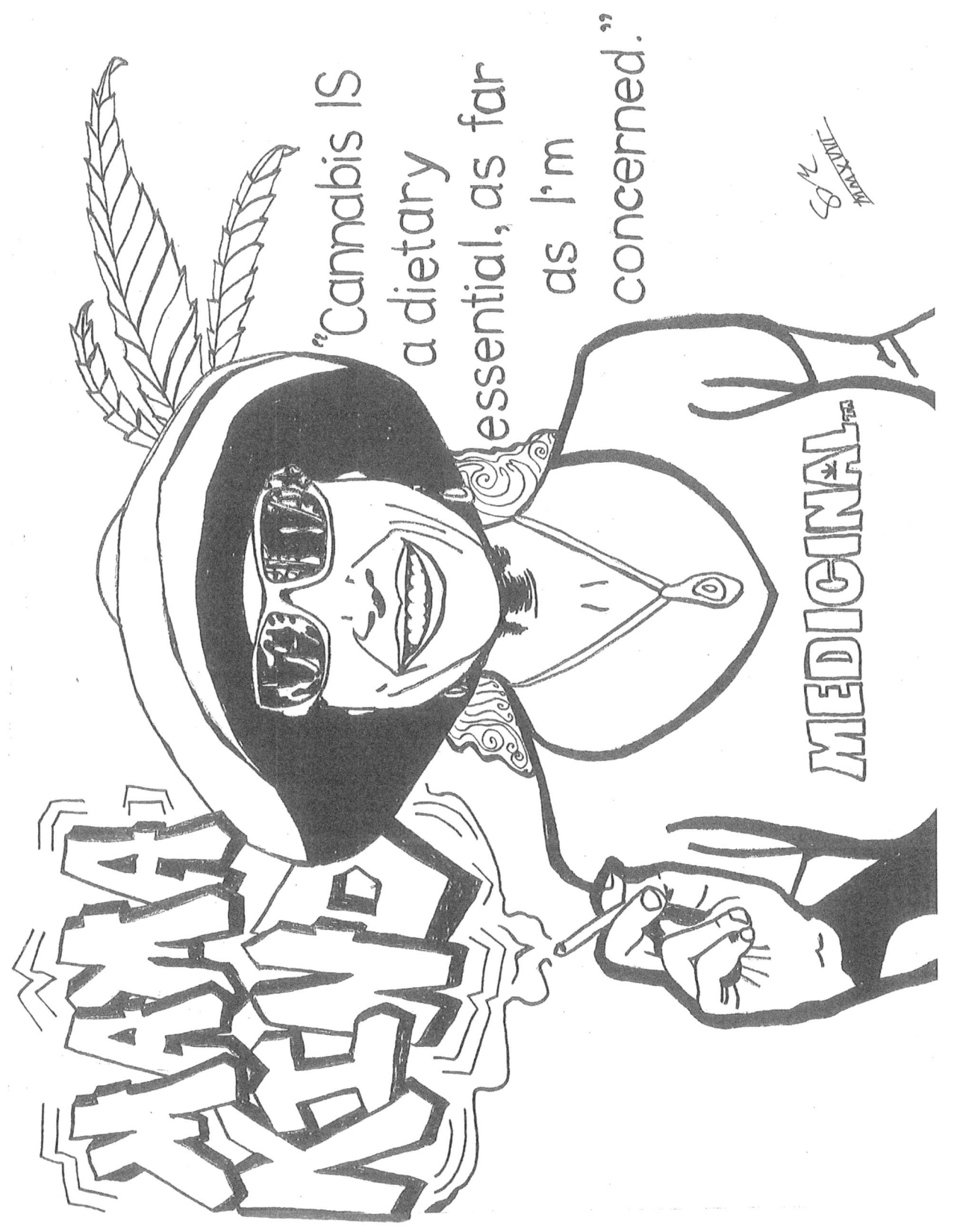

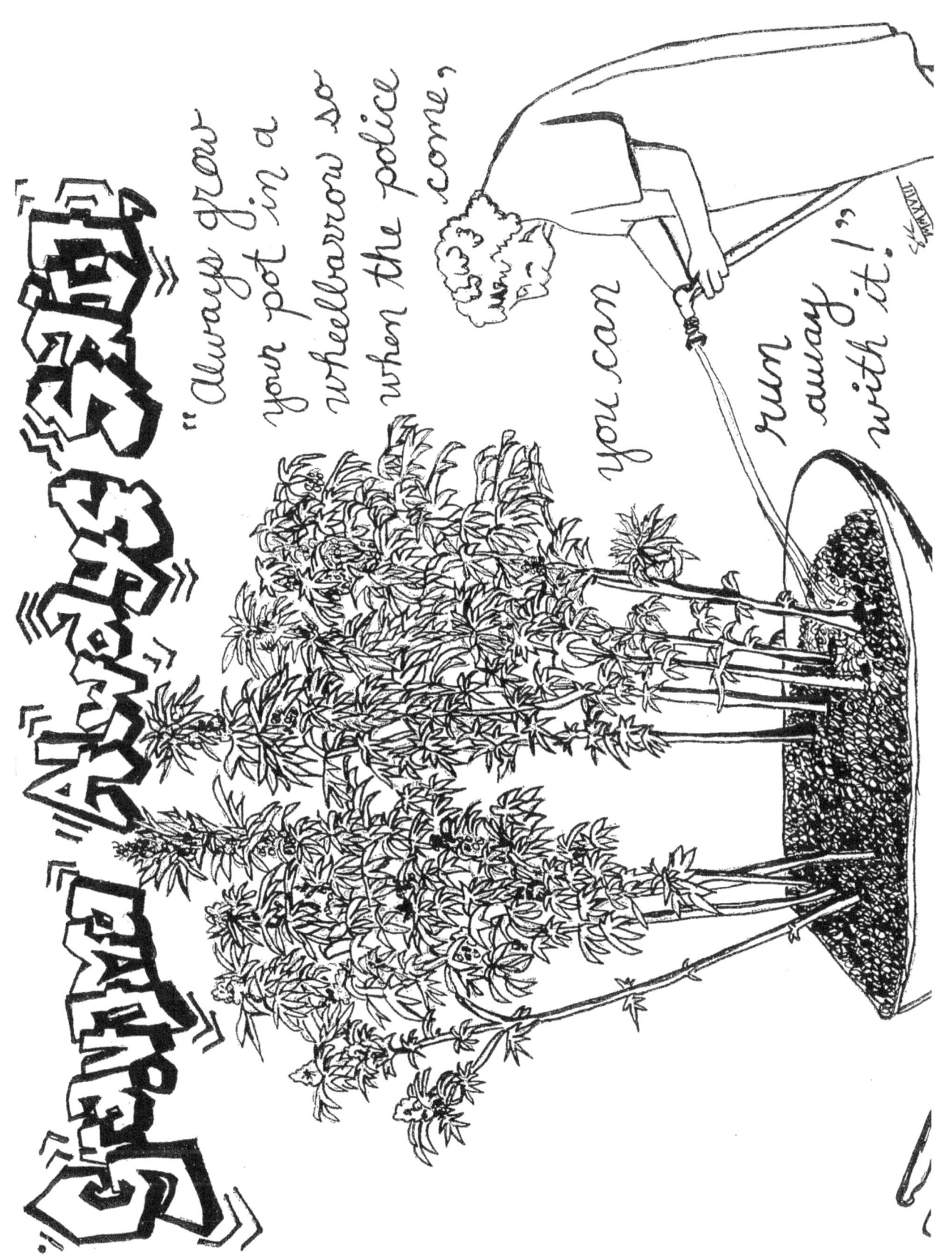

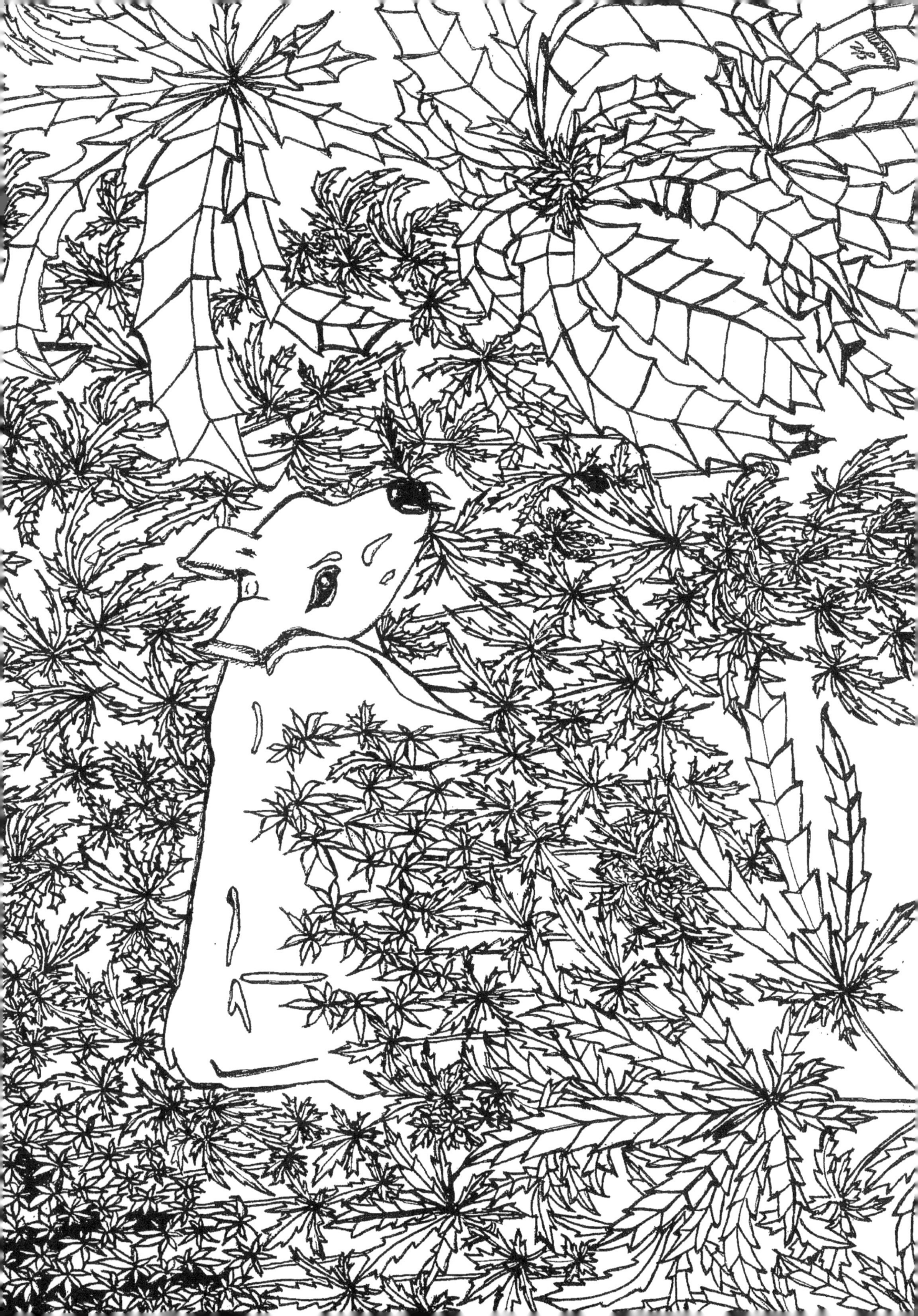

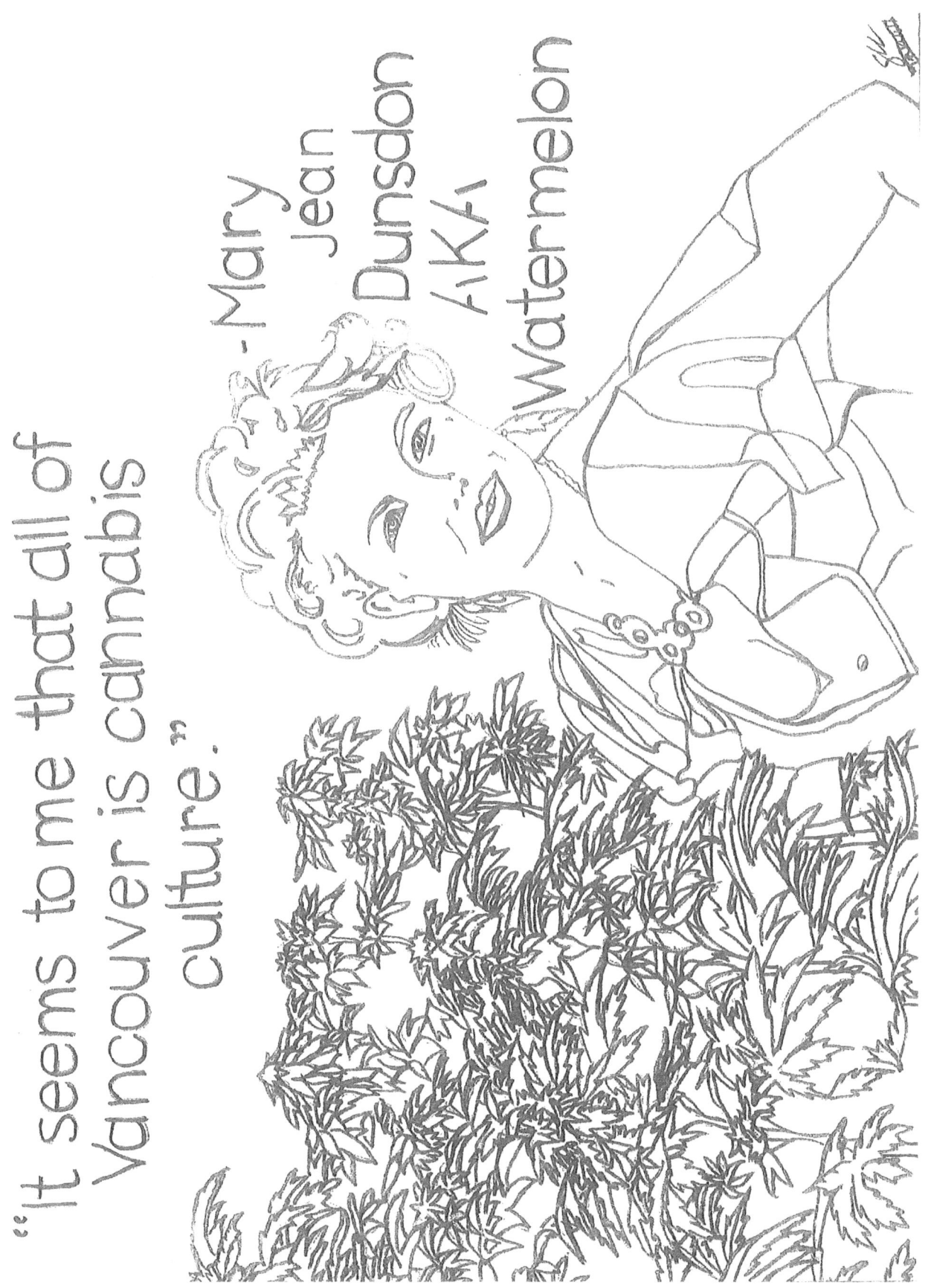

"It seems to me that all of Vancouver is cannabis culture."

-Mary Jean Dunsdon AKA Watermelon

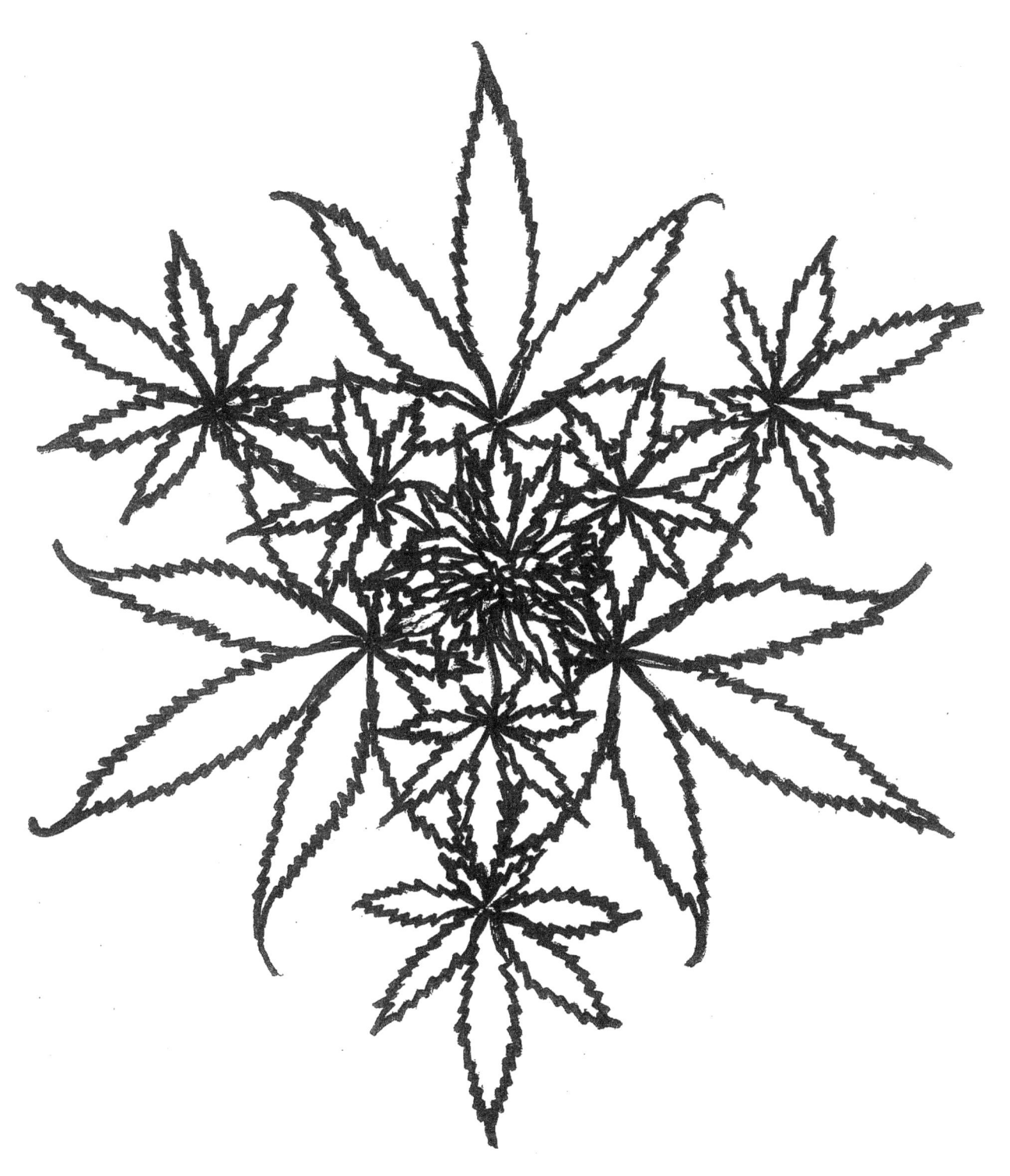

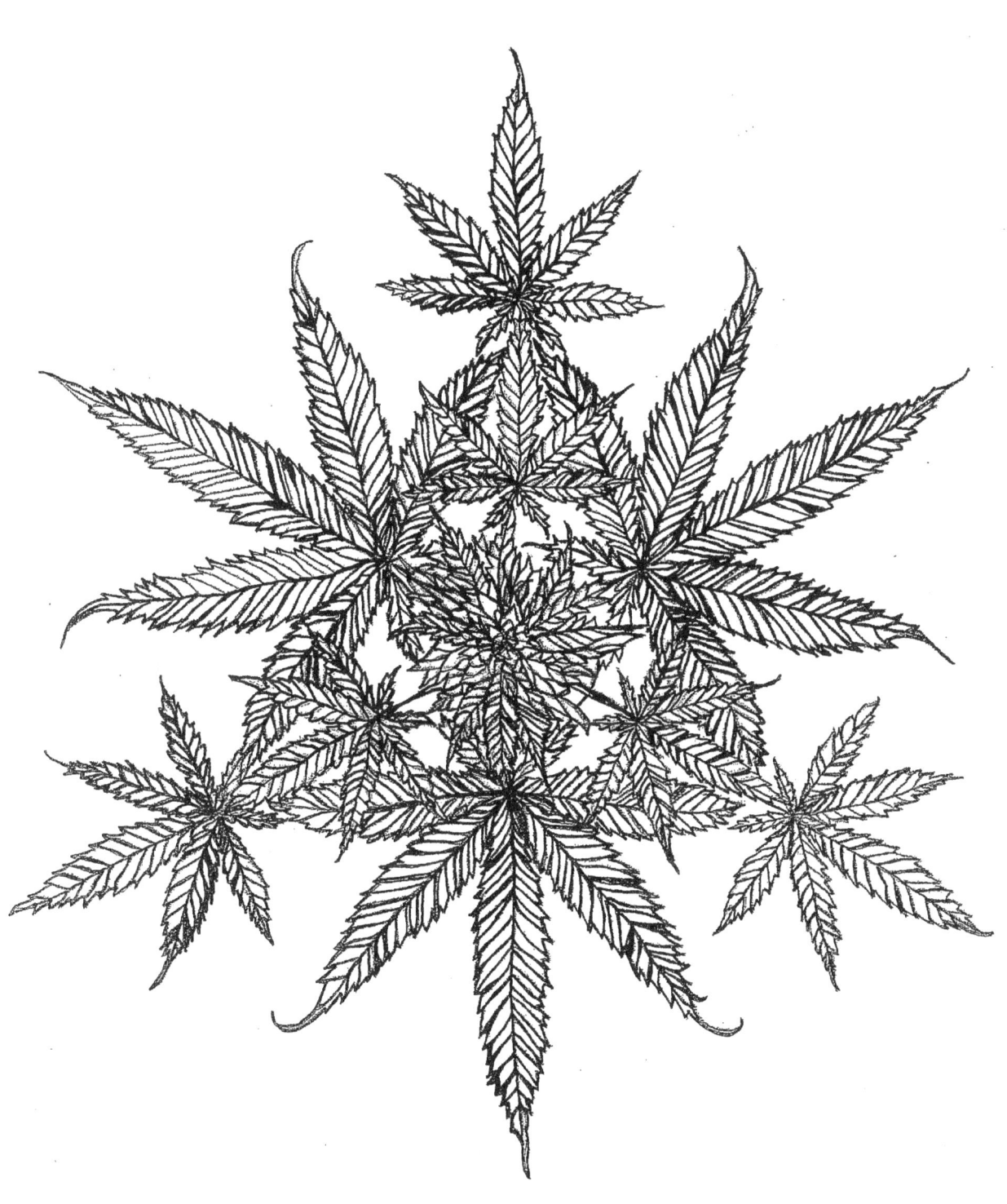

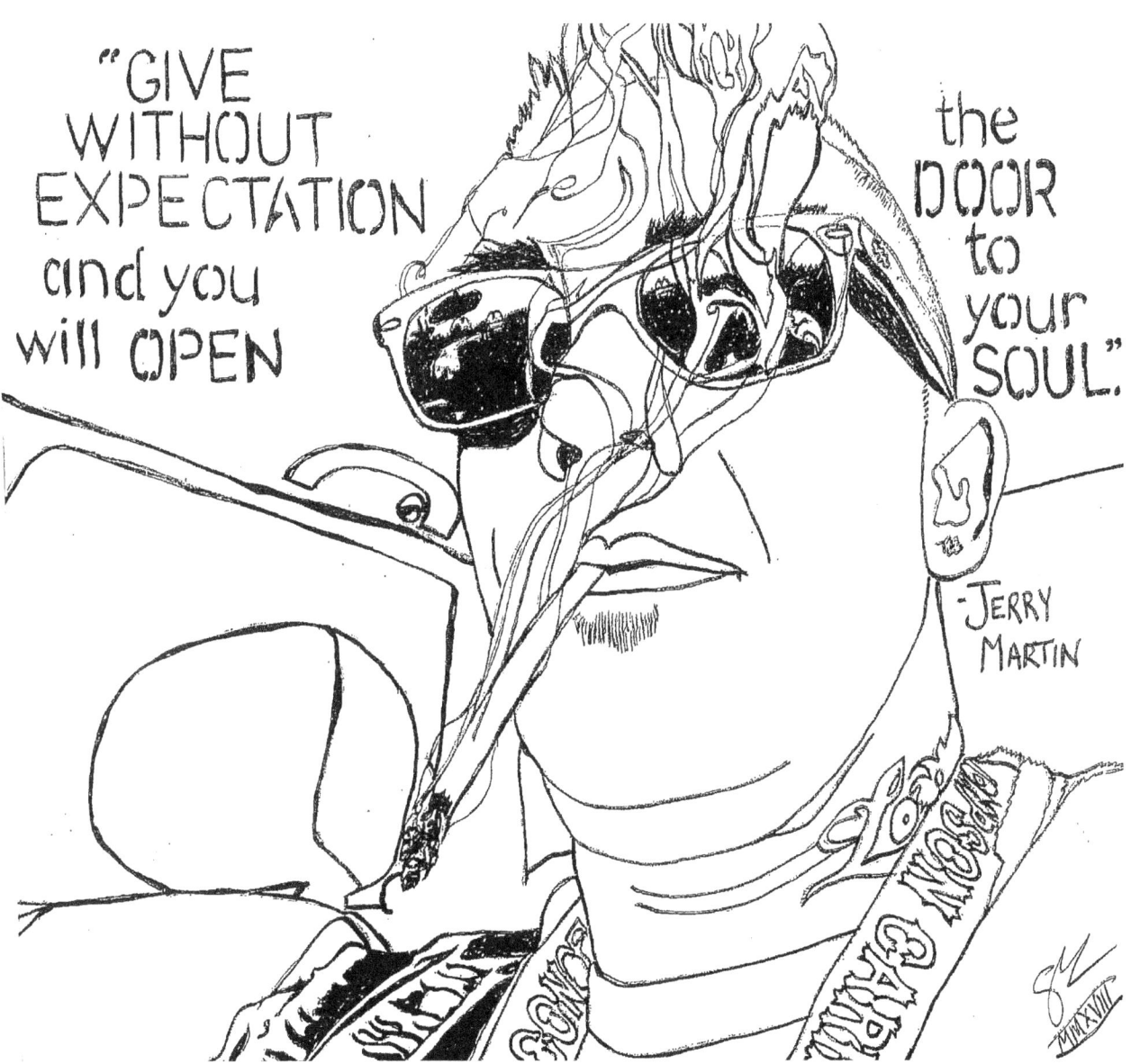

"GIVE WITHOUT EXPECTATION and you will OPEN

the DOOR to your SOUL."

-JERRY MARTIN

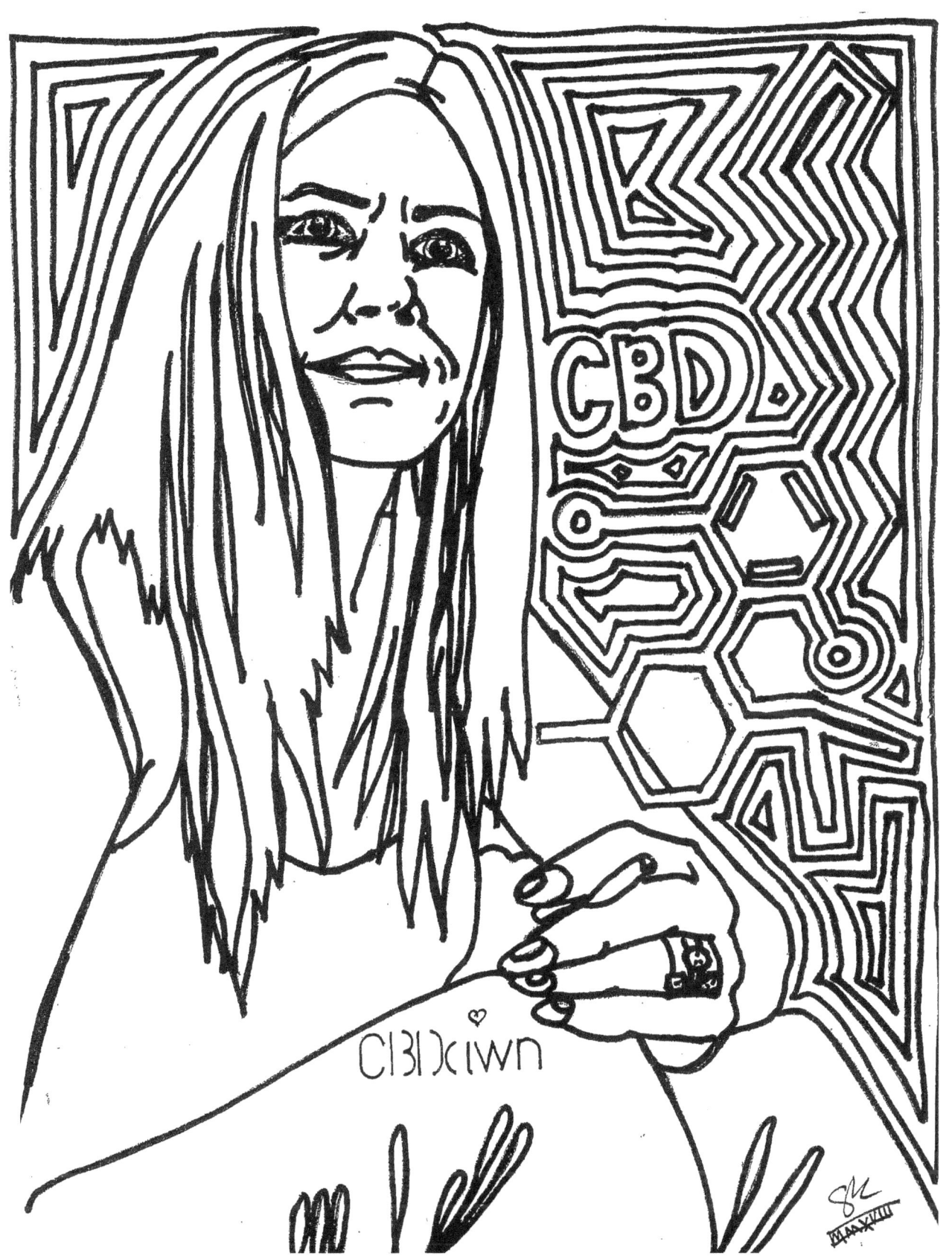

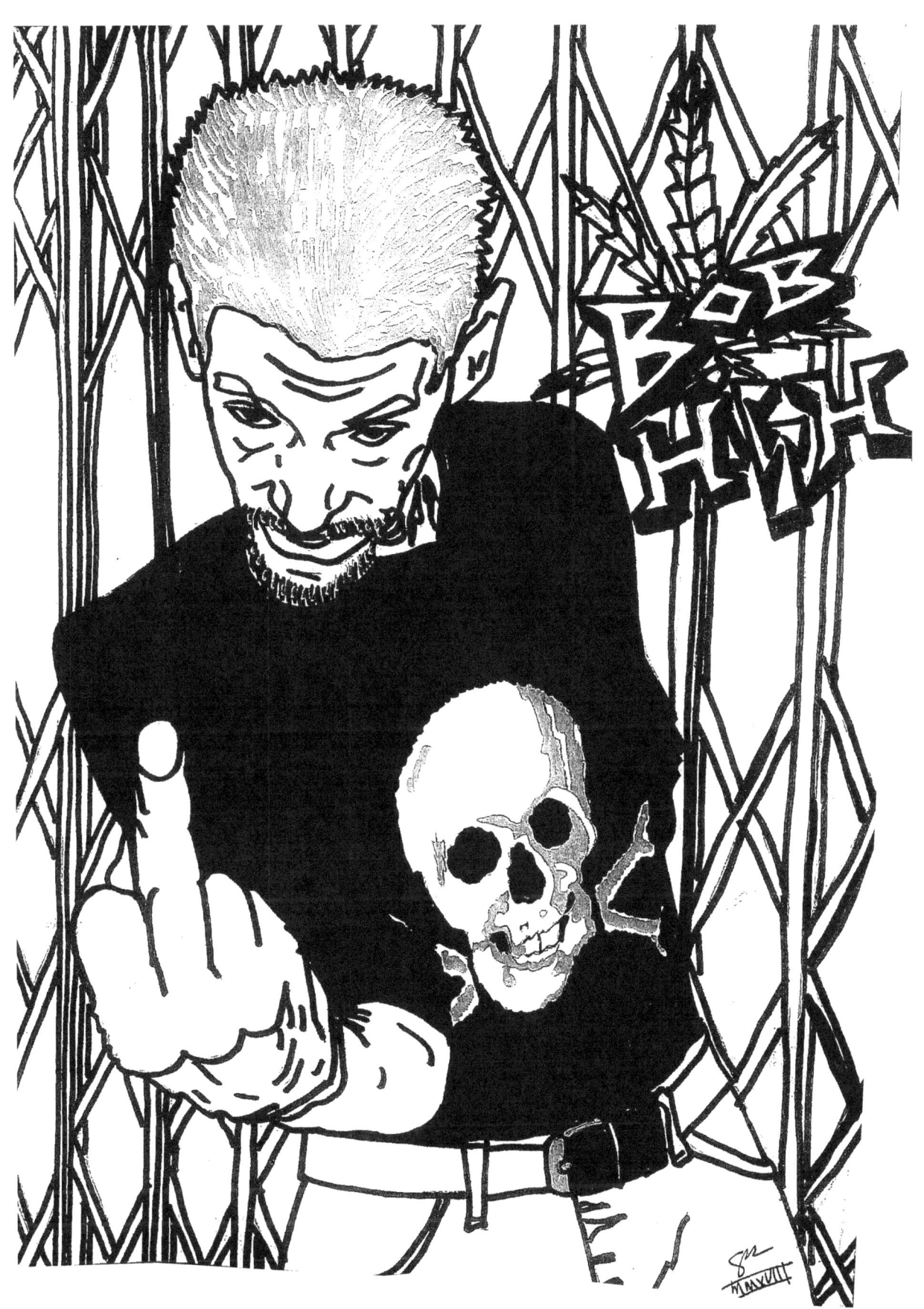

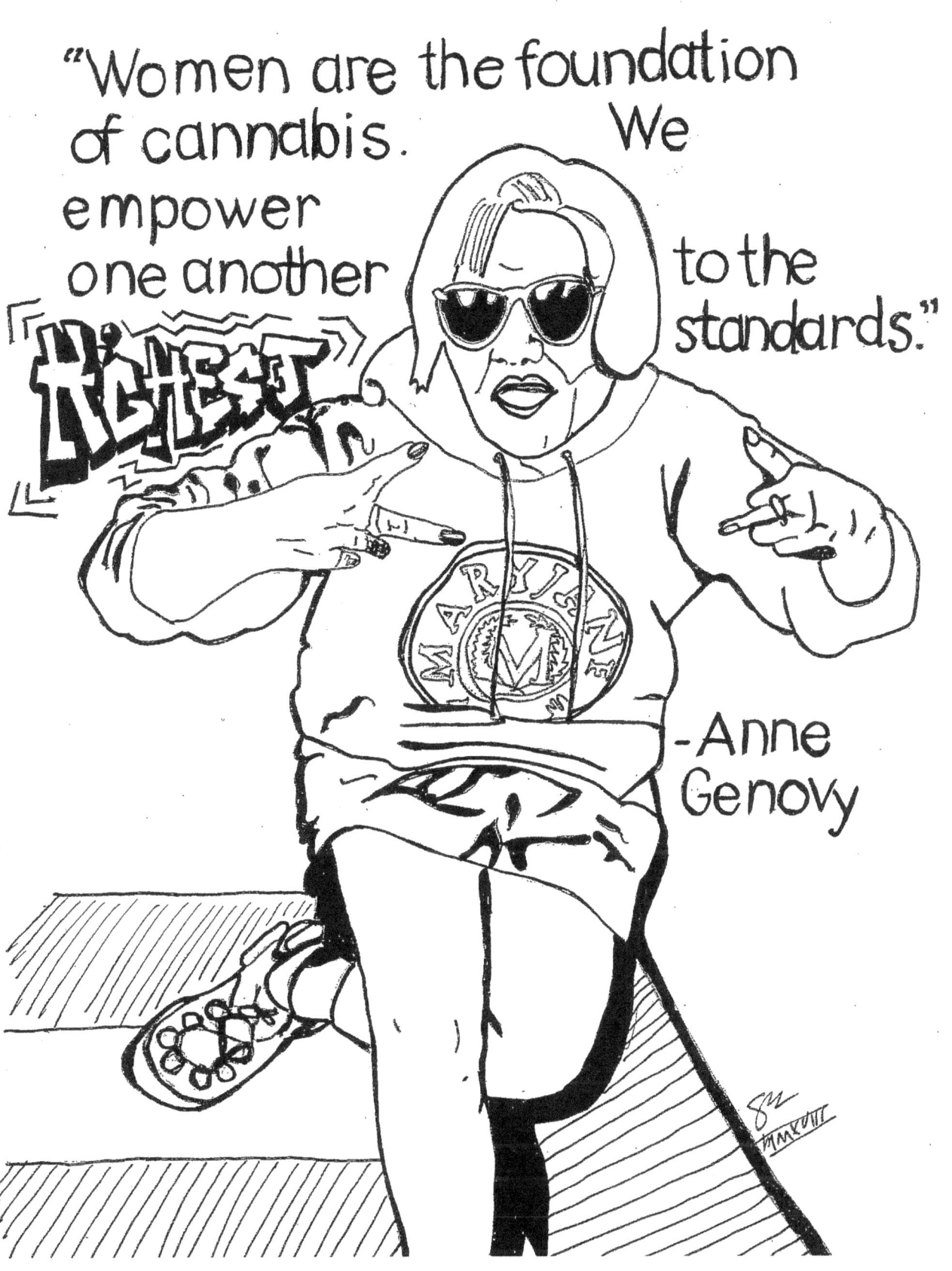

"Marijuana is a wonder drug because it is remarkably non-toxic - on a par with coffee with respect to both dependence and toxicity."

- Dr. Lester Grinspoon, Harvard Medical School

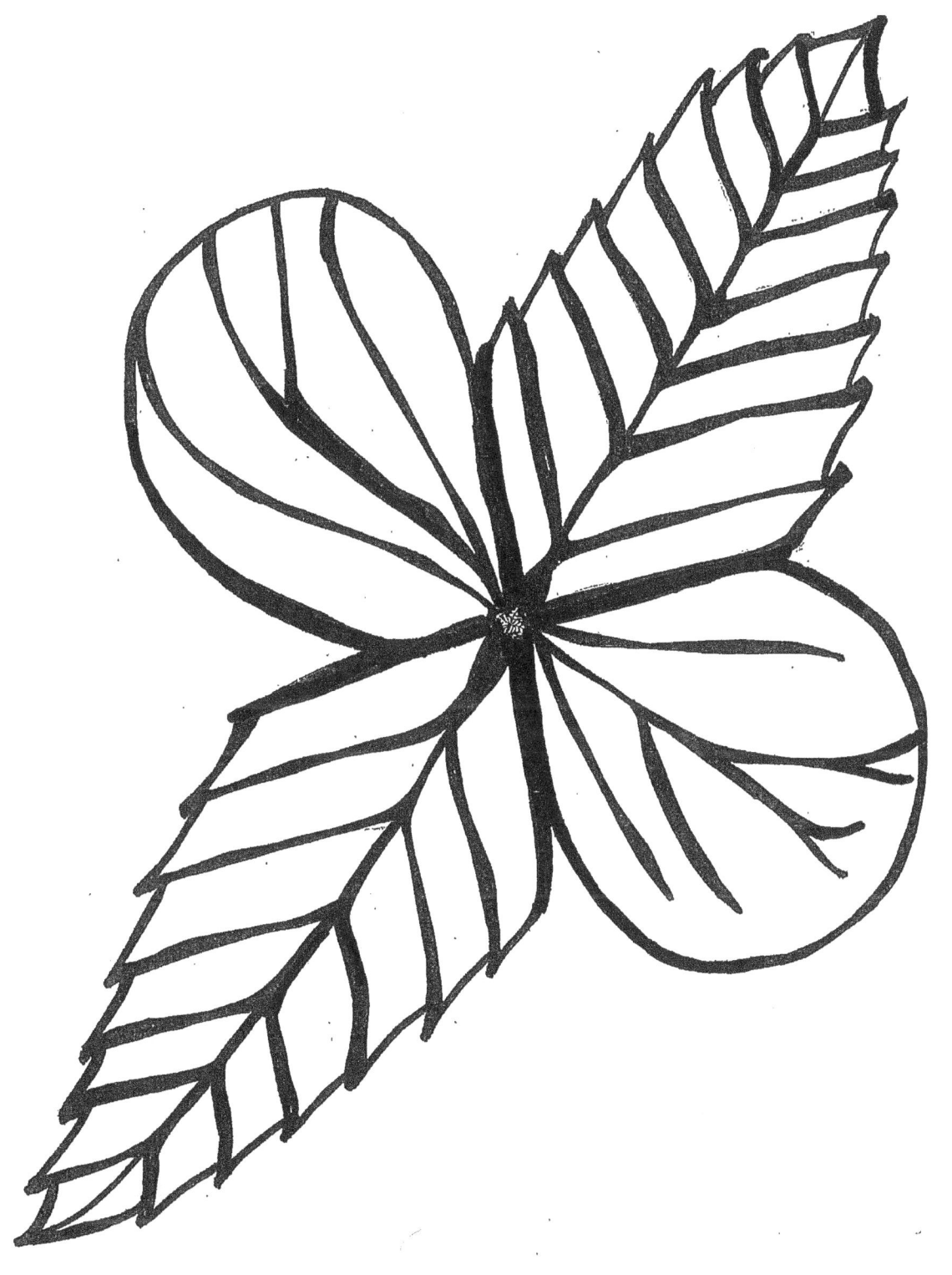

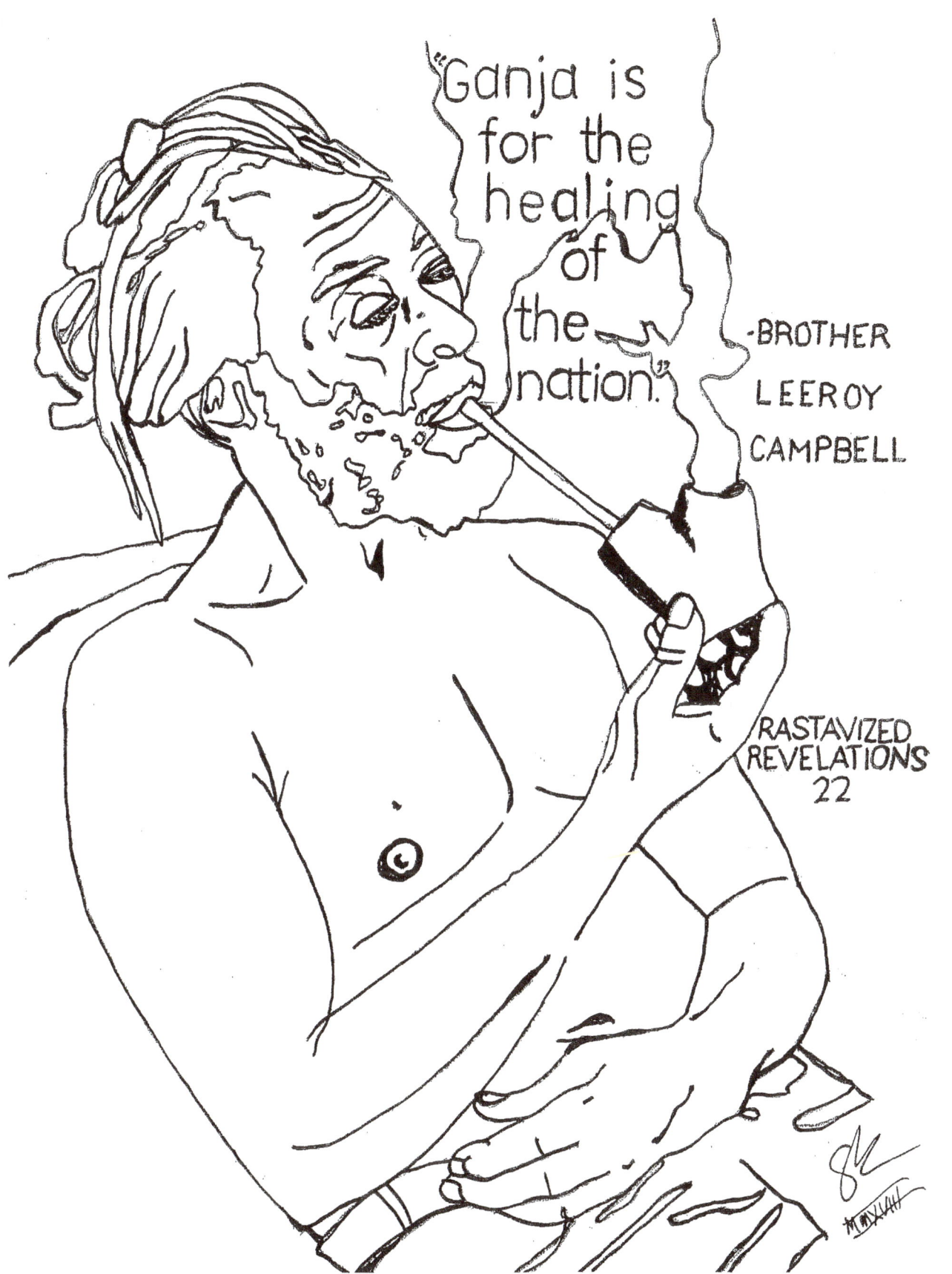

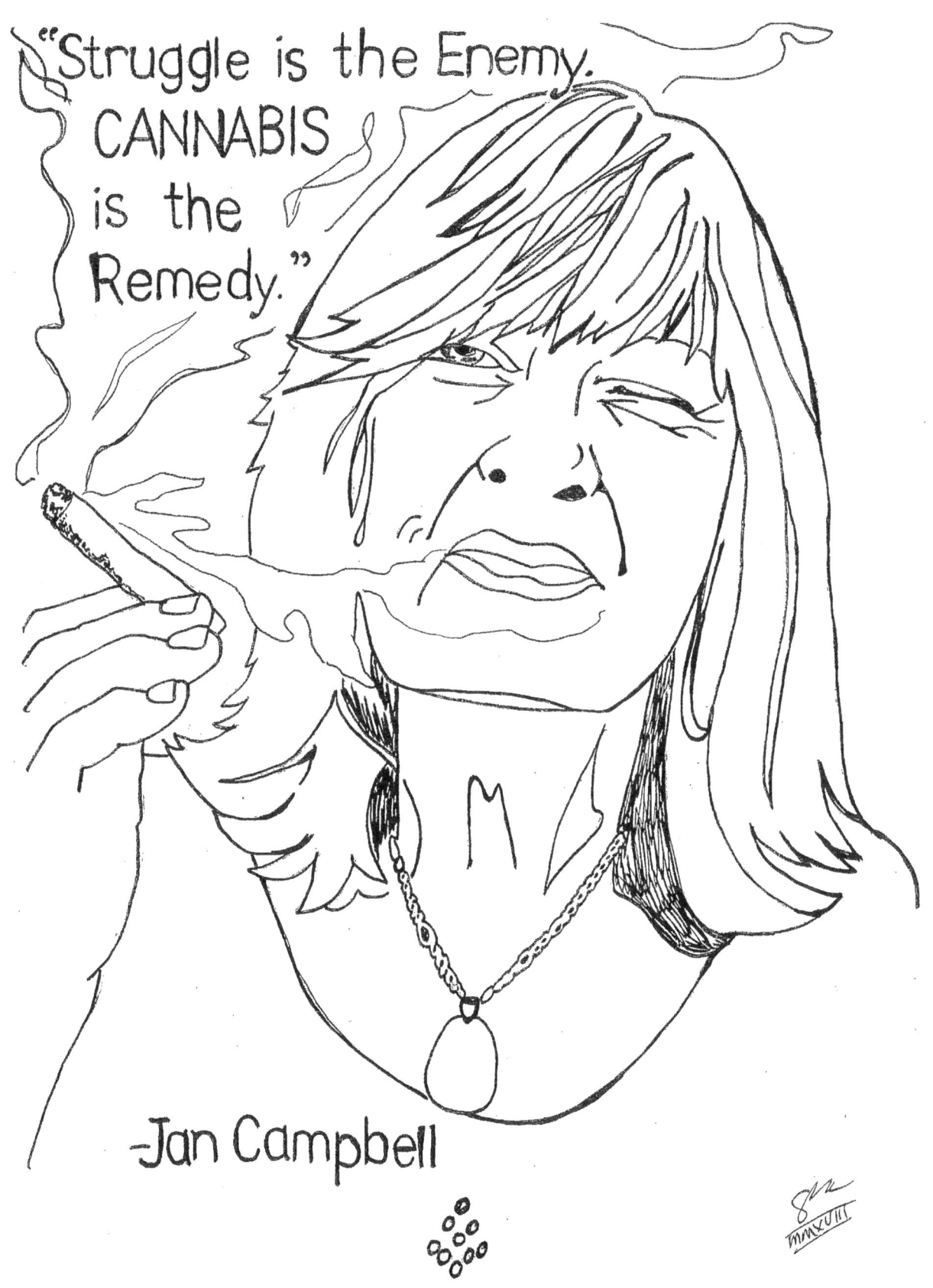

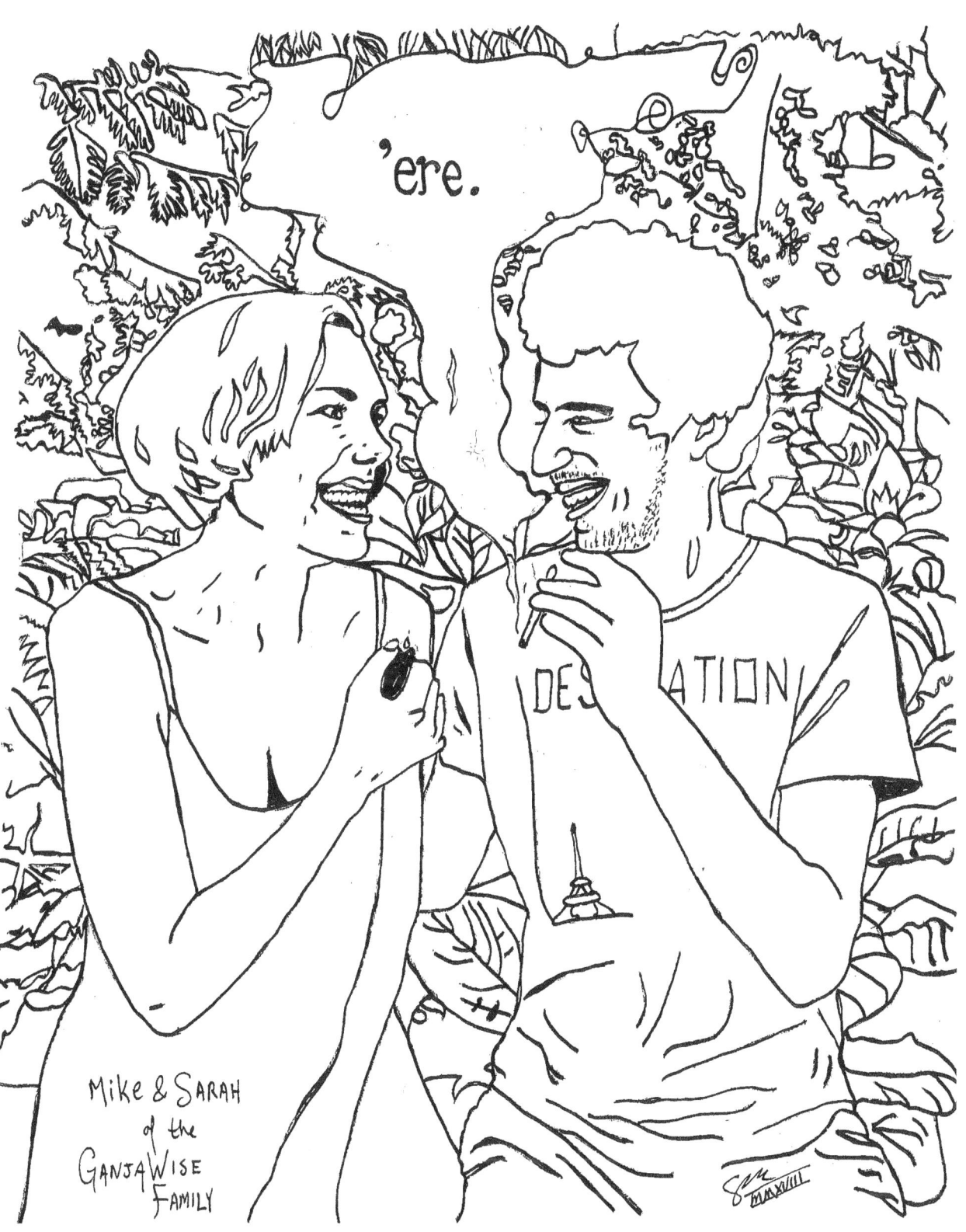

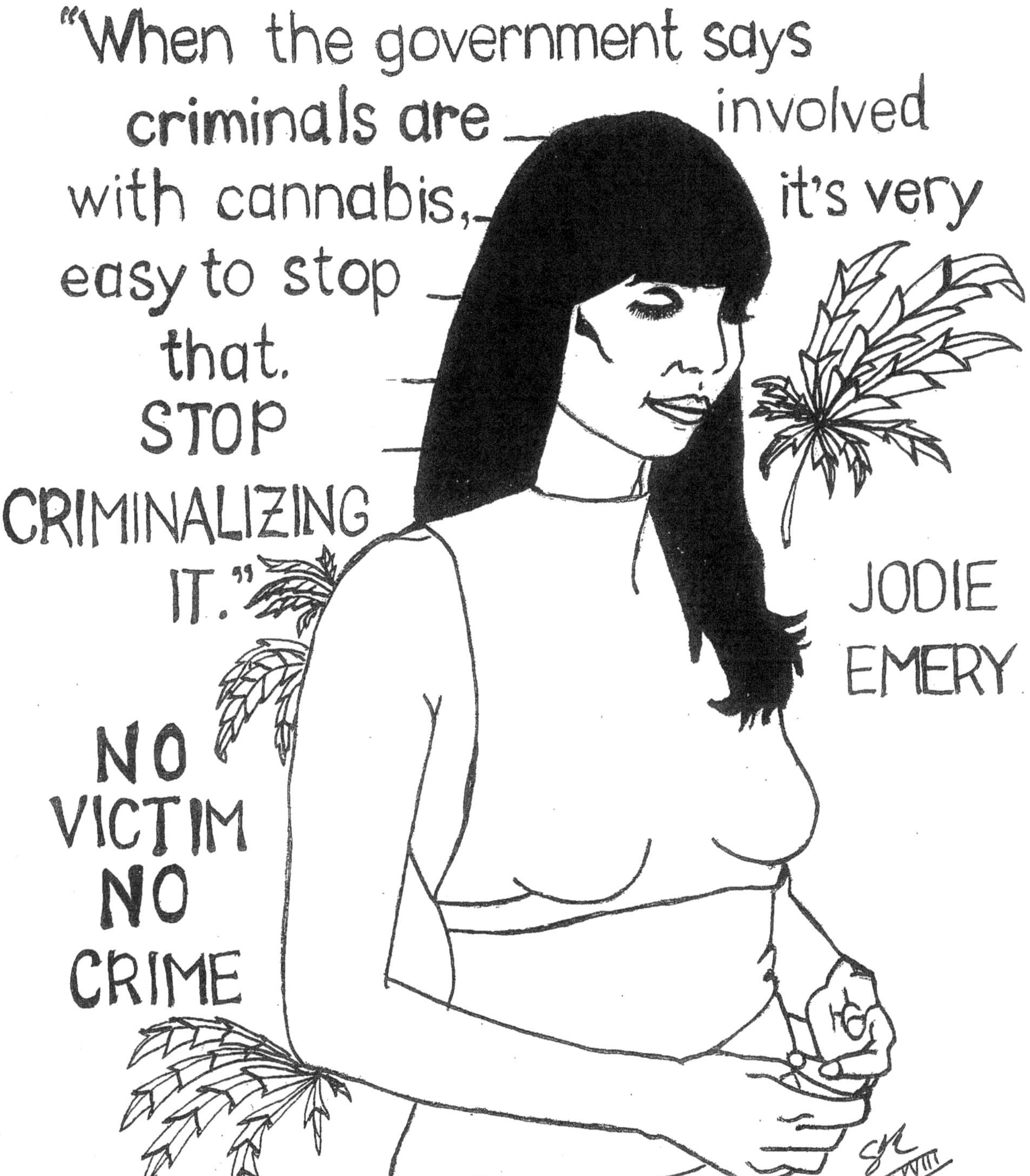

"When the government says criminals are _____ involved with cannabis, _____ it's very easy to stop _____ that. STOP CRIMINALIZING IT."

JODIE EMERY

NO VICTIM NO CRIME

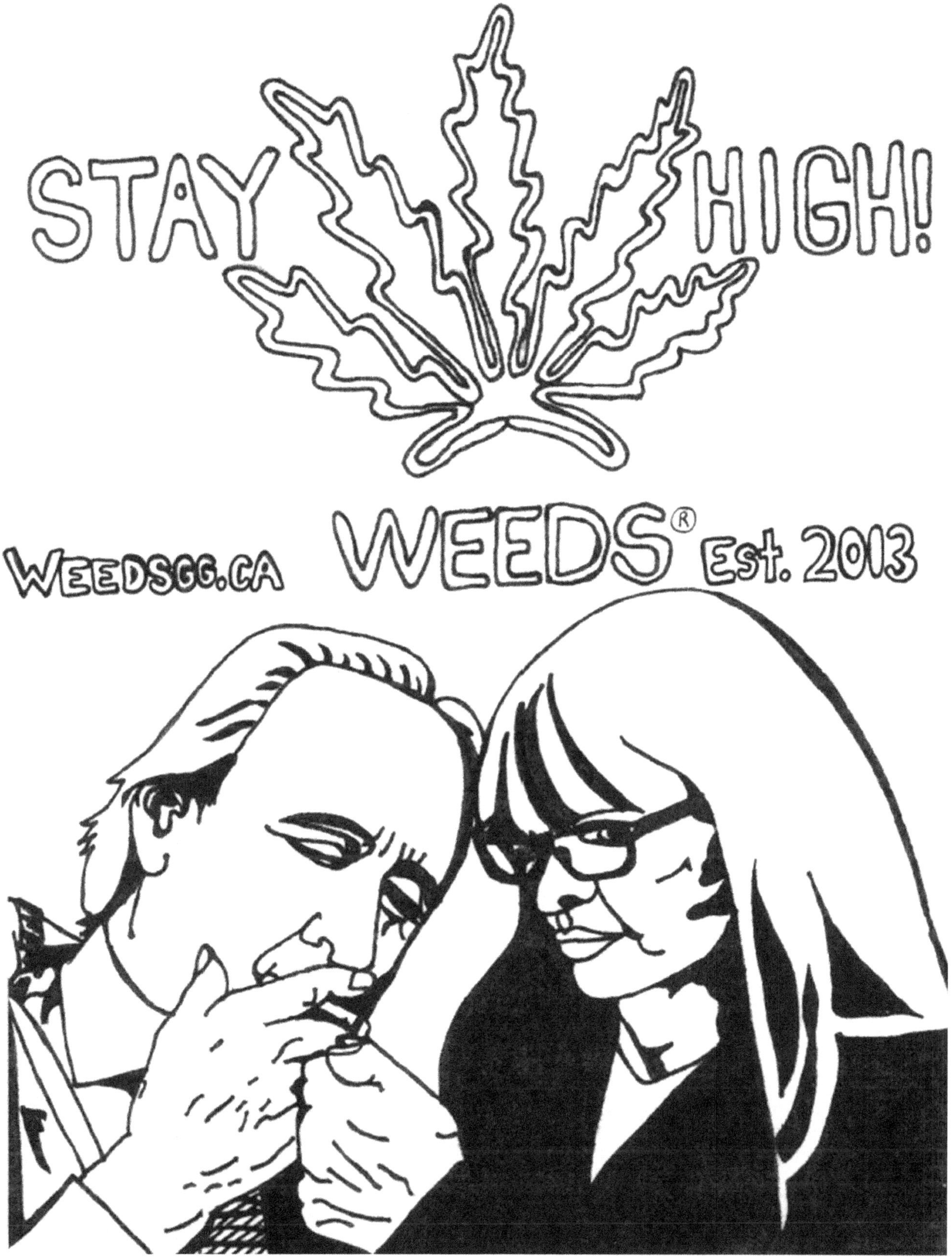

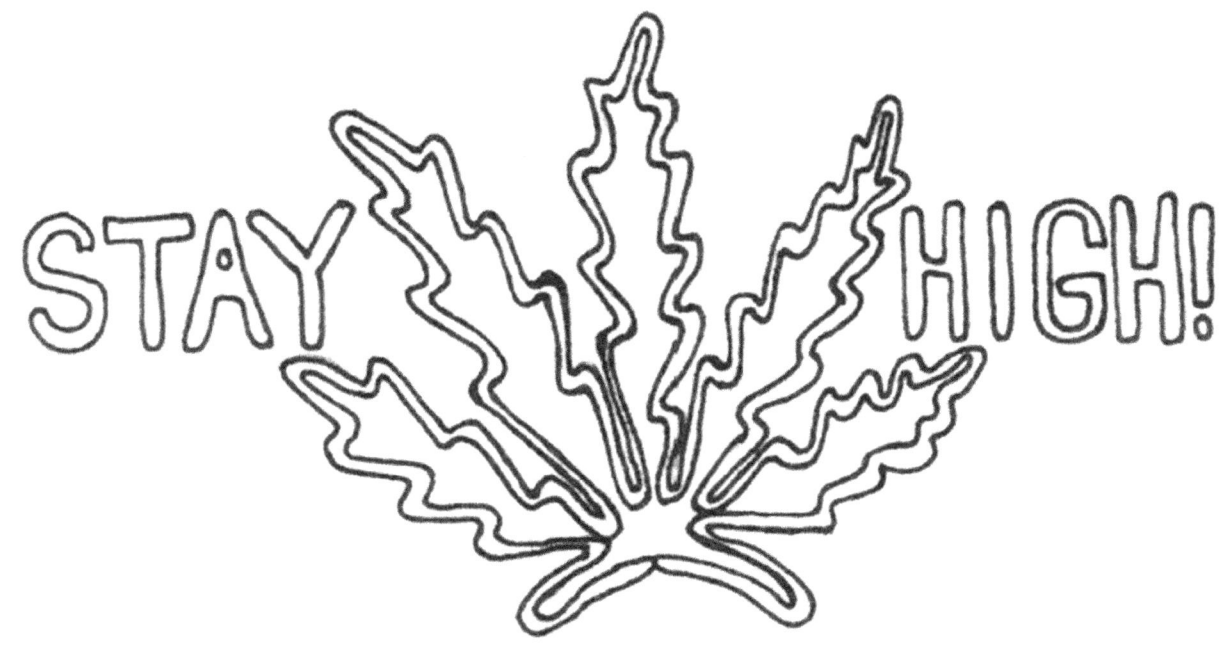

STAY HIGH!

WEEDSGG.CA WEEDS® Est. 2013